the Mythic Goddess Tarot

Channel the power of sacred femininity for insight into the past, present, and future

Jayne Wallace

CICO BOOKS
LONDON NEW YORK

Acknowledgments

Many thanks to my partner Lee Ryan, publisher Cindy Richards, editors Carmel Edmonds and Slav Todorov, designers Emily Breen and Jerry Goldie, Gordana Simakovic in production, and the sales and design team at CICO Books for bringing great ideas into being. Thanks to Hannah Davies for her wonderful illustrations, my brilliant team at Psychic Sisters, Selfridges, and my agent Chelsey Fox. Special thanks to Lucy Hunter for content and inspiration.

Published in 2022 by CICO Books
An imprint of Ryland Peters & Small Ltd
20–21 Jockey's Fields   341 E 116th St
London WC1R 4BW   New York, NY 10029

www.rylandpeters.com

10 9 8 7 6 5 4 3 2 1

Text © Jayne Wallace 2022
Design © CICO Books 2022
Illustrations © Hannah Davies 2022

The author's moral rights have been asserted. All rights reserved. No part of this publication may be reproduced, stored in a retrieval system, or transmitted in any form or by any means, electronic, mechanical, photocopying, or otherwise, without the prior permission of the publisher.

A CIP catalog record for this book is available from the Library of Congress and the British Library.

ISBN: 978-1-80065-155-5

Printed in China

Commissioning editor: Kristine Pidkameny
Senior commissioning editor: Carmel Edmonds
Editor: Slav Todorov
Senior designer: Emily Breen
Art director: Sally Powell
Production manager: Gordana Simakovic
Publishing manager: Penny Craig
Publisher: Cindy Richards

Contents

Introduction 4
Getting to Know Your Cards 5
Beginning a Reading 5
Finishing a Reading 6

The Spreads 6
One-card Reading 6
Past, Present, Future 6
The Power Pyramid 7
The Crossroads 8
The Celtic Cross 9
The Divine Truth 10

The Major Arcana 11
0 Eos: The Fool 12
I Hekate: The Magician 13
II Seshat: The High Priestess 14
III Asase Yaa: The Empress 15
IV Ma'at: The Emperor 16
V Juno: The Hierophant 17
VI Aphrodite: The Lovers 18
VII Diana: The Chariot 19
VIII Aiyélála: Justice 20
IX Persephone: The Hermit 21
X Tyche: The Wheel of Fortune 22
XI Athena: Strength 23
XII Dhumavati: The Hanged Man 24
XIII Ragana: Death 25
XIV Bao Gu: Temperance 26
XV Ananke: The Devil 27
XVI Pele: The Tower 28
XVII Elpis: The Star 29
XVIII Selene: The Moon 30
XIX Magec: The Sun 31
XX Rhiannon: Judgment 32
XXI Lakshmi: The World 33

The Minor Arcana 34
The Four Suits 34
The Elements 34
The Suit of Wands: Fire 37
The Suit of Swords: Air 44
The Suit of Pentacles: Earth 51
The Suit of Cups: Water 58

Introduction

One of the things I love about goddesses is that they are everywhere. From every corner of the globe, you will find mythologies, stories, and fables with gods and goddesses at their heart. Whether in ancient Greece, Africa, Asia, or Europe, or with any type of religion, it's easy to see throughout history the impact these superhuman beings have had on the shaping of the world we know today.

There are variations in these tales, of course, but there are plenty of overlaps, too. This makes you consider what it is about gods and goddesses that makes people living anywhere from Africa to the Arctic come up with remarkably similar explanations of the world. Is it possible that at a spiritual and primal level these explanations carry truths about us as humans?

Traditionally, gods have encapsulated all that is good about masculinity—the strength and bravery of Greek mythology's Hercules or Thor in the Norse tradition. Of course, they often possess other attributes, too, such as being angry and harsh in the case of Zeus or Hades. Goddesses, on the other hand, have been celebrated for their beauty, love, sexuality, motherhood, creativity, and fertility—but dig a little deeper, and you can see these divine beings also embody inner strength, courage, ingenuity, and wisdom.

We can see humanity's hive mind at work quite easily in the relationships between Roman and Greek divinities—Venus and Aphrodite, for example. Indeed, there are love goddesses everywhere—Jiutian Xuannü from China, Oshun from West Africa, and Áine from Ireland, to name just a few.

Anthropologists have proposed the theory that many thousands of years ago we became capable of imagining a world beyond that which we had seen and experienced. We understood our communities would continue after each individual death, so we began to tell stories, to weave a belief system. Much of this was intended to explain the physical realities of the world, which shaped early humans' fates. Each tribe and community had their own stories, but, somehow, humanity's collective psychic consciousness came up with remarkably similar narratives with stories, characters, and rituals, all of which helped us make sense of the world. We all know these tales—a mixture of tragedies, comedies, overcoming monsters, exploration, quest, rags to riches, and rebirth.

The mythic sagas provide encouragement as we struggle to survive difficulties. Gods and goddesses provide both warnings and inspiration when it comes to dealing with life's challenges. The tarot carried on this tradition when it was developed in the fifteenth century. Tarot experts have linked the Major Arcana with the "hero's journey" story—the first card, the Fool, starts off on a path through life's challenges and mysteries. This journey has also been recognized as a pattern in mythology.

We use the tarot to access the wisdom of the collective unconscious. Linking the tarot to humanity's original stories makes for a deck that is magical.

Let us begin our journey...

Getting to Know Your Cards

Before reading with this deck, you need to connect with its energy and form a sacred bond with your cards. You can do this by going through the deck and touching each card, or sleeping with the deck under your pillow for a week. You could also pick an individual card to focus on each day, thus gradually familiarizing yourself with the whole deck. Once you've connected with your deck, you can start reading with your cards.

Beginning a Reading

Begin by finding a quiet place and creating a relaxing atmosphere by lighting candles or burning incense. Look through the Major Arcana part of the book (pages 11-33) and discover which goddess you feel most drawn to. You do not have to read the text—let yourself be led by gut instinct. Chant out loud or in your head:

"Goddess [name of goddess], reconnect me to my highest self. Grant me wisdom, awaken me to my inner truth."

Choose a spread you feel drawn to (pages 6-10) and hold the deck with both hands. Shuffle the cards and start to breathe slowly and deeply. As you do this, ask the cards to provide you with help and insight during your reading, and focus on everything you want to ask. If you are reading for someone else, ask them to think of the question and focus on their energy. If you or the person you are reading for don't have a specific question, simply ask the cards for any helpful guidance or reassurance that they can provide.

Do this for a few moments and spread the cards face down in a fan shape, selecting those you feel most drawn to until you have the number you need for your chosen spread. You can do this either with your eyes open, or by closing your eyes and gently moving your hands over the deck and seeing which cards your hands naturally gravitate toward. If you are reading for someone else, spread the cards and ask them to pick the ones they feel drawn to. Alternatively, you can cut the deck into three piles and choose the one you feel most guided to. Gather the other two piles together and place your chosen pile on top; then, when selecting the cards, draw from the top of the deck.

Place the remainder of the deck to one side and turn the chosen cards over one at a time. Trust your gut reaction to each card and pay attention to any names, places, or images that pop into your mind.

Once you have finished the reading, thank the cards for their insights and guidance, and give them a final shuffle to clear their energy. Extinguish any candles and incense you've used and place the cards back in the box or a drawer until you want to use them again.

Introduction 5

Finishing a Reading

This light meditation will help you close yourself down psychically after a reading. It can take as much or as little time as you like, and it's also a great technique for helping you relax and switch off at the end of the day.

Begin by sitting comfortably in a quiet room while holding your cards and lighting a candle to help you relax. Close your eyes and deepen your breathing. Do this for a few moments until you feel completely calm and serene.

When you're ready, start to visualize a white light glowing around you, gently going through your body, and warming each part individually. Focus on each area separately, and feel a wave of relaxation going through your body.

Take a few more deep breaths and then imagine a beautiful green light appearing around your heart. Visualize it becoming clear in your mind and focus all of your energy on its color. Affirm: "I thank my cards for their guidance and their wisdom."

Once you've done this, picture the green light gradually becoming smaller until it completely disappears. Take a deep breath and visualize yourself being placed in a bubble of protective energy until your next connection.

The Spreads

The following spreads will help you get started on your tarot journey. If you're new to tarot, try starting with some of the simple spreads, such as the one-card reading below, then move on to the longer ones when you're feeling more confident. Alternatively, choose the spread you feel most drawn to and which you feel would be most helpful for you or your querent (person who consults a tarot reader).

One-card Reading

This classic one-card spread is ideal for times when you need a quick answer to a question, or would simply like some guidance for the day ahead. You can also use this technique to pick an inspiring affirmation to focus on each day.

Find a quiet space and take a few deep breaths until you feel calm, centered, and relaxed. Shuffle the cards and ask for any guidance or insight they can provide for the day ahead. Alternatively, if there's a specific question you would like to ask, repeat it several times in your head.

Now select your card using your preferred technique (see page 5). Once you've chosen your card, turn it over and look up its interpretation. Make a note of the card and its interpretation in a journal, and also jot down anything else that pops into your mind. Even if it doesn't make sense to you now, it may later on, so it's always worth writing it down.

Past, Present, Future

The time-honored three-card layout is a wonderful way of exploring your—or your querent's—past, present, and future. You can either focus on a particular issue or ask the cards for general insight into the influences affecting you and your life at a particular time.

The first card symbolizes the past and will highlight any previous events that have led you to your current situation or are still affecting you now.

The second card represents the present and focuses on the issues influencing your life today and how to navigate your way through them.

The third card, indicating the future, will suggest the likeliest outcome based on how things are now. But remember, this is by no means set in stone. It can change depending on your free will and your actions, so don't be too disheartened if the outcome isn't what you were hoping for.

Begin by shuffling the deck and asking for insight

Past **Present** **Future**

into your past, present, and future. Select three cards using your preferred technique (see page 5) and lay them out as shown above.

Turn them over one at a time and interpret their meanings based on their positions in the spread.

The Power Pyramid

The three-sided form carries a deep spiritual symbolism. The ancient Egyptians recognized this when they constructed the pyramids, which served as tombs of the Pharaohs.

The pyramid's three sides may have been designed to catch the rays of the sun, which in turn would have helped the king's soul ascend to heaven to join the gods, particularly the sun god Ra. Other theories propose that these were powerful healing chambers, deriving mystical strength from the power of three. The triangle represents a higher perspective. It can be understood to mark the cycles of growth that lead to a higher state of being.

In this three-card spread, all cards carry equal importance, like the three sides of a pyramid. Without all three, the whole structure collapses.

The Power Pyramid spread is great for checking in on yourself or your querant emotionally. You can use each side to represent the following:

- 1. Mind, 2. Body, 3. Spirit
- 1. Physical, 2. Emotional, 3. Spiritual
- 1. What I think, 2. What I feel, 3. What I do

1. Mind

2. Body **3. Spirit**

Select your cards using your preferred technique (see page 5), lay them out one by one, and begin your interpretation.

The Spreads 7

The Crossroads

When we find ourselves at a crossroads in life, it can feel daunting. Indeed, the origin of the word crisis is crossroads (from the Greek "choose" or "decide"). Of course, not every moment we are required to choose a path is a crisis in the modern sense of the word, but it's unsurprising that we reach for our tarot decks when we are faced with a crossroads.

In Greek mythology, crossroads are associated with Hekate, so it's appropriate to call upon this magical goddess to ask for help when doing this layout. Say:

> "O Hekate, goddess of crossroads,
> keeper of knowledge,
> guide me through the shadows
> and enlighten me to my destiny where
>   I can flourish."

Now select the cards using your preferred technique (see page 5) and lay them out. Cards 4 and 5 represent what will happen if you take specific paths. Turn them over one by one and begin your interpretation.

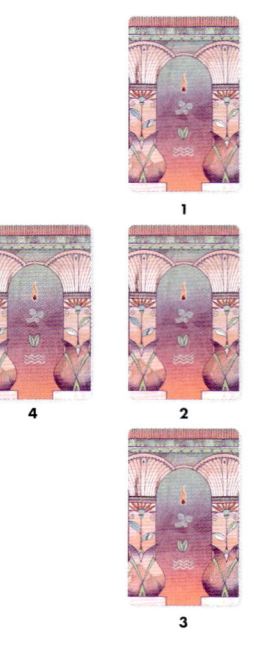

1. Your motivation
2. Ideal outcome
3. Your values
4. Option 1 likely outcome
5. Option 2 likely outcome

8 The Spreads

The Celtic Cross

If you wish to go deeper than a one- or three-card spread, and you are looking for more of a psychological approach to a tarot reading, the Celtic cross can give you wisdom and guidance.

The Celtic cross tarot is believed to have been used for centuries across the British Isles. One theory suggests that it's based on the stone pillars topped with crosses found in Ireland, a place where the old spirituality and the new have entwined seamlessly.

What the Celtic cross offers isn't a quick fix. It's best for those who are willing and able to take a long view of life, spiritual progression and growth. The lessons may not be easy, but what's more challenging can ultimately be more rewarding.

The general shape is divided into two sections. The cross shape represents a current issue, how it came to be, and where it may lead. The pillar gives greater depth and understanding of the background, aiding the querent to gain better insight into the situation.

Select your cards using your preferred technique (see page 5), lay them out one by one, and begin your interpretation.

Card 1: The present
Card 2: The challenge
Card 3: The past
Card 4: The future
Card 5: The best outcome
Card 6: Subconscious motivations
Card 7: Advice
Card 8: External influences
Card 9: Hopes and fears
Card 10: Likely outcome

The Spreads 9

The Divine Truth

The world of gods and goddesses was one way our ancestors made sense of the world around them. Another way was through the recording of time, or the phases of the moon with its ever-changing form giving rise to the concept of the month, with a new moon often seen as a time of renewal, and a full moon associated with culminations and fulfillment.

A 12-month tarot spread is a way to get an overview of your year and prepare for any joys or challenges that may come your way. You can use it as a general tarot spread, or meditate on particular areas, such as asking about love, career, or family, or anything that you wish. Do keep in mind that the 12-month tarot spread gives a snapshot of the probable course of the following year. It won't trump free will, and situations can alter.

Select your cards using your preferred technique (see page 5), lay them out one by one, and begin your interpretation.

1. Month 1 (current)
2. Month 2
3. Month 3
4. Month 4
5. Month 5
6. Month 6
7. Month 7
8. Month 8
9. Month 9
10. Month 10
11. Month 11
12. Month 12
13. Overall Year

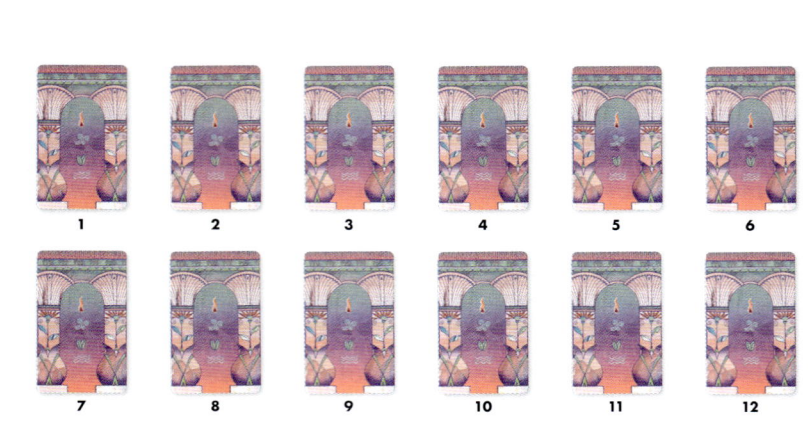

10 The Spreads

The Major Arcana

One of the first things you notice about any tarot deck is that there are two types of card: the Minor Arcana and the Major Arcana. The Minor Arcana consists of 56 cards divided into four suits, like playing cards. The Major Arcana consists of 22 cards, each with its own distinctive archetype and meaning, as well as its own spellbinding tale.

The Major Arcana takes us through the hero's journey, from the beginning (the Fool's card), right through to completion of a phase and fulfillment (the World). Along the way, there is all human experience—our highs and lows, our pleasures and our pain.

Uncertainty and withdrawal are reflected by the Moon and Hermit cards. Joy and success are signified by the Sun and the Wheel of Fortune. Each card is associated with a mantra that you might want to chant as you pick up the card. Keywords will guide you to choose the card most suitable for a particular reading.

Just like the stories of the ancient gods and goddesses, we can see our triumphs and struggles mirrored within the Major Arcana. Most importantly, each experience and each card offers us a learning opportunity—even, or perhaps especially, the cards we may fear, such as Death or the Devil.

Using the interpretations on pages 12-33 you will discover from the goddesses which message and learning experience they hold for you. You can gain insight into the universal world of mythology and humanity's shared magical wisdom.

You might want to begin learning about the tarot by initially using only the Major Arcana. When you are ready, you can incorporate the cards in the Minor Arcana into your readings.

0 Eos: The Fool

KEYWORDS: Fresh starts, innocence, zest for life

Eos is the golden Greek goddess of dawn, suffused with joy and the possibility of the new, robed in saffron-dyed gold, orange, and crimson. Every morning, at dawn, she rises into the sky from the river Okeanos and opens the gates of the sky with her rosy fingers so that her brother, the sun god Helios, can ride. Eos's very presence is powerful; as she rises at the start of each day, radiating rays of light, the demons of the night flee. Known as a free spirit who takes lovers as she pleases, she had a son, Memnon, an Ethiopian king, who was killed by Achilles. Zeus, one of Eos's lovers, resurrected Memnon and granted him immortality.

MEANING: Optimism Eos represents the start of something potentially quite wonderful. Traditionally, women would petition her for assistance with fertility and new romantic entwinements. Eos offers the twin benefits of wisdom and certain protections against the demons of doubt. Eos is all about hope—her radiance even saved her son. You are at the start of an exciting, unexpected new adventure. Yes, this may involve a gamble, but sometimes a little risk is necessary, so we can move on and grow as people. Be brave! This card signals possibilities such as new relationships and projects, pregnancy, opportunities, travel, and job offers.

Take a leap of faith on a brand-new journey.

I Hekate: The Magician

KEYWORDS: Skill, duality, manifestation

Known as the queen of the crossroads, Hekate is the chief Greek goddess presiding over magic and spells, and represents the thin veil between life and death. Through Hekate, the spirit world and humans can dance. Her powers can unlock all mysteries and she is a shapeshifter. It is said that Hekate once served as a messenger for the other deities. She stole the goddess Hera's beauty to give to her rival, Europa. Hera chased Hekate, who fled first to the bed of a woman in childbirth, then to a funeral procession, and finally to Lake Acheron in Hades, where she was cleansed. Hekate emerged more powerful than ever, a goddess of birth, death, and purification. She witnessed the abduction of Demeter's daughter Persephone to the underworld and, torch in hand, rescued her back.

MEANING: Power Hekate is a goddess of life, death, regeneration, and magic ... and her powers can aid you. If you find yourself at a crossroads, literal or metaphorical, say her name and she will respond with subtle signals—after all, with her torch she can bring light. Hekate is telling you that you have the power within you to succeed and reach your dreams. Expect magical happenings—stumbling across the right knowledge or person, seemingly unexpectedly. Love is bringing exhilarating surprises, too. Whatever situation you're in, harness your full potential and take action. You will have to make a choice, but Hekate and her mystical abilities are within you to ignite thrilling transformation.

I am all that I need, both inside and outside.

The Major Arcana 13

II Seshat: The High Priestess

KEYWORDS: Intuition, mystery, higher self

Egyptian goddess Seshat is expert in the art of sighting the stars and planets and calculating astronomical and astrological measurements for the location of temples. She is closely connected with Thoth, her brother, lover, and husband. He invented writing, but Seshat invented letters. It is said that when an author creates a story, inscription, or book on earth, a heavenly copy is transferred to Seshat, who places it in the library of the gods; mortal writings transform to immortal. Seshat is said to record the names of dead souls, revive the deceased in the afterlife in preparation for their judgment, and assist their souls to move on toward the hope of paradise.

MEANING: Hidden talents Seshat is the keeper of knowledge, both in this life and the next. Among her many skills, ultimately it is Seshat's spiritual power to help us move on to the next realm that is her most impressive superpower. She is showing you now that it is time for you to listen to your intuition, rather than logic or intellect. Seshat is the holder of information—and of secrets. She invokes enlightenment, inner illumination, divine knowledge, and wisdom, and offers encouragement that you are on the right path. Listen to your dreams—your psychic powers of understanding are enhanced now. Secrets are about to be revealed ... Seshat encourages us to use creativity and collaboration to make the most of this new information.

Inner knowledge is my best guide of all.

III Asase Yaa: The Empress

KEYWORDS: Truth, fertility, rebirth

Asase Yaa is the beautiful, mysterious goddess worshipped by the Bono/Akan people of West Africa and beyond. Asase Yaa is the wife of Nyame, the sky deity, who created the universe. She is Mother Earth—Asase translates as "Earth" and Yaa means "female born on Thursday." Asase Yaa gave birth to humanity, so she represents new life. Offerings and toasts are made in her name and she is linked with fertility, agriculture, and the cycle of life, and called upon for protection during a child's naming ceremonies. She is known as the upholder of truth and peace. There are many stories linked to Asase Yaa, including how she is adored by Twe, a spirit from the water. He vows to give fish to her at any time. All she has to do is touch the water. We can show Asase Yaa respect by respecting the earth—if we do this it will yield to our needs.

MEANING: Abundance New beginnings and rebirth are on the horizon. Fertility is starred—this may be in the literal sense with a new baby. If you're not ready for this, it could be time to take precautions! This card can also represent a new romance or venture. Like Asase Yaa, all you need to do is to give a wish your touch—with a little bit of effort, you should obtain a successful outcome. Express yourself creatively with arts, music, or writing. Money and resources should become plentiful, and a move of home into a better property may happen now. A positive new relationship could be on the horizon. Good fortune surrounds this card, and you should feel joy that Asase Yaa is caring for and guiding you.

Connecting to the earth reminds me that abundance is unlimited.

The Major Arcana 15

IV Ma'at: The Emperor

IV Ma'at: The Emperor

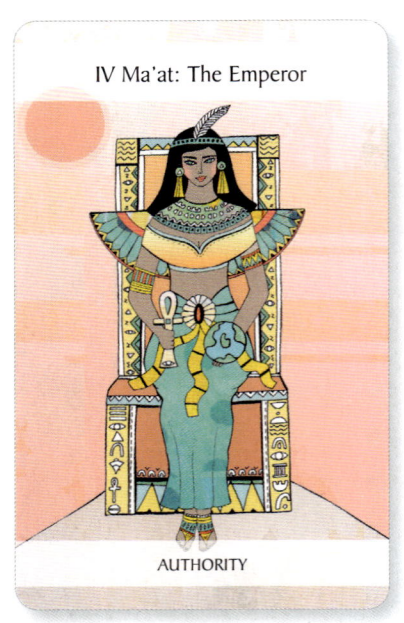

AUTHORITY

I am my own authority. My moral code creates my own life's structure.

KEYWORDS: Wisdom, inner moral compass, clarity

Ma'at is the Egyptian goddess of truth, order, and natural ethical and moral law, the spirit of what is right versus what is merely legal or lawful. Most importantly, she upholds order. Ma'at was created when her father, Ra, arose from the waters of chaos. She was married to Thoth, god of wisdom. Ma'at's existence kept everything in balance, offering morality and justice. In ancient Egyptian mythology, after the death of the body, everyone had to pass through the Hall of Judgment, where a person's heart, which contained a record of all their actions in life, was weighed on a scale against Ma'at's feather of truth. If the person's heart balanced with Ma'at's feather, they could continue their journey to the afterlife. If not, that person was denied eternal life.

MEANING: Authority Ma'at represents a righteous moral code, which links with the divine and the soul. Ma'at represents leadership, and fosters honor and discipline. A decision may be needed that requires you to act rationally, with integrity and for the greater good. Promotions, achievements, and deserved accolades may well be coming your way. You could be taking on a leadership role where you can command and direct others. You are clear-eyed when it comes to manifesting your goal, and you have the strength to stand up and say and do what is right. Remember—you're in charge, you have the final say. You have the power and moral authority to settle disagreements now. In love, this card can represent involvement with someone older or who possesses great wisdom.

V Juno: The Hierophant

KEYWORDS: Learning, tradition, union

Juno, the Roman goddess of marriage, is the protector of the state and guardian of tradition. She is known as the Spirit of Time, in charge of organizing the orderly division of time. In this capacity, she rules the menstrual cycle, the earliest calendar. Matron and protector of women, Juno has the power to fulfill any request made by a devotee. Although she is often equated with the Greek goddess Hera, Juno is calm, regal, and serene, unlike the volatile Hera. Juno is a guardian, alert for her charges' safety. Legend has it that her sacred geese gave warning to the Roman military when the Gauls tried to invade Rome.

MEANING: Spiritual wisdom Juno personifies tradition and she was celebrated throughout the traditional Roman calendar as the focus of several major festivals. Juno is suggesting you look to tried-and-tested ways of doing things—they could offer answers and protection. Perhaps family traditions have fallen by the wayside and your heart is yearning for them. Juno is also alerting you to new knowledge, so keep alert for opportunities. Is there someone around you whom you respect, who you can learn from? A teacher, mentor, or guide could be arriving in your life and offering structure and principles, or you could be joining a respected group or institution. Study and gaining respected knowledge are all highlighted by this card. Serious commitment, especially in the form of marriage, may happen soon.

I choose which traditions I embrace, and how I do it.

The Major Arcana 17

VI Aphrodite: The Lovers

KEYWORDS: Soulmates, choices, bonds

Aphrodite is the Greek goddess of love, beauty, desire, and all aspects of sexuality. A seductress and the most desired of all women, she could tempt both gods and men into her boudoir with her incredible powers of attraction. Aphrodite is the daughter of Zeus and Dione, although some accounts have her created from Uranus's genitalia. This duality perhaps represents the high and base forms of love and sexuality. Love is complicated—and so is Aphrodite. She had many admirers, but married Hephaestus, a god who also worked as a blacksmith. Out of all her many suitors, he was considered by the gods the ideal candidate to settle with Aphrodite. Hephaestus was overjoyed to be married to the goddess of beauty and forged beautiful jewelry for her, including a girdle to flatter her womanly body, making her even more irresistible.

MEANING: Love Aphrodite is offering you perfect union, harmony, love, and attraction—this card is all about finding the right balance. Aphrodite's beauty was a blessing, but with so much on offer for her, finding the perfect equilibrium was her quest. Love, unsurprisingly given Aphrodite's symbolism, is likely to be a key matter for you now. Relationships may become stronger and move to another level, but if a union is weak or troubled, it could be time to explore new possibilities. This card is not just about romance. Vital decisions are now being considered in life, in finances, and at home. You may be facing something of a dilemma as you ponder and weigh up your options. Only you can make the call, but take care and don't just settle for whatever is easy. The road less traveled may turn out to be the right direction.

I embrace love and happiness.

VII Diana: The Chariot

KEYWORDS: Determination, willpower, direction

The Roman goddess Diana is a huntress. Known as a rebel goddess with a spirit of independence, Diana was associated with slaves, immigrants, and those living on the margins of society. The fact that she didn't have it easy from the start could explain this kinship. Diana was born after the god Zeus took advantage of her mother, Leto, leaving her pregnant with twins. Zeus's wife, Hera, cursed Leto so that no land or sea—no place under the sun—would give her a place to rest and give birth. By chance, Leto's sister Ortygia had been turned into a floating island that rose above the sun. This loophole offered sanctuary—a floating island was neither land nor sea. Leto gave birth to Diana smoothly, but Apollo, her twin, caused terrible labor pains. It was up to infant Diana to act as a midwife to her own brother.

MEANING: Success Right from the moment Diana drew breath, she had to fight and take charge to help her mother and brother survive. Diana is with you now, offering strength and confidence to help you overcome challenges and triumph, whatever the odds. You are striving to achieve your goals—and you can do exactly that, but you must maintain focus, determination, and a certain boldness and stubbornness. The solution to the seemingly insurmountable is within you. Even if your personality is on the gentle side, it's time to show your teeth. We shouldn't fear being competitive and ambitious. Courage and grit are within you. Take charge of your own destiny. With the right attitude, you can win.

I have the power— no obstacles can stop me.

VIII Aiyélála: Justice

KEYWORDS: Fairness, truth, cause and effect

Aiyélála was a real woman, but her true name is shrouded in secrecy. Her story begins with a man from the Ilaje tribe in West Africa who'd had an affair with a nobleman's wife—a transgression punishable by death. Another tribe, the Ijaw, granted him sanctuary, which led to a bitter dispute. After mediation, the Ilaje demanded that the adulterer, or a substitute, must die. An enslaved woman was summoned to be the proxy. Rather than meekly accepting her fate, all this woman could do was repeat the word "aiyélála," which translates as "the world is incomprehensible," about the injustice of her fate. Aiyélála has become a symbol of social morality and justice and worshippers pray to her for righteousness and retribution.

MEANING: Justice Aiyélála's tale initially appears to be more about injustice—a blameless woman sacrificed to pay for the lust of a man. Yet it is this woman's cry that has endured; it is she who is now venerated as a goddess, a kind of karmic righting. Aiyélála's journey is about the search for truth. If you are seeking justice, this card offers a positive sign. However, perhaps things are not as clear-cut as on first glance. Keep aware and look at the whole story when deciding what is true and fair. In terms of your own behavior, is there something you will be judged for? Look to your motivations—have you behaved in accordance with your own moral code? If you have acted with honor, things will fall into place. If your actions have been lacking in integrity, you may need to be accountable for this, but bringing things into balance in this way can lead to resolution.

Justice is truth in action.

IX Persephone: The Hermit

KEYWORDS: Soul-searching, meditation, inner guidance

Persephone—the beautiful daughter of Zeus, the chief Greek god, and Demeter, the goddess of agriculture—was pursued by Hades, king of the underworld. Zeus knew Demeter would never agree to the match, so it was arranged secretly. Hades snatched Persephone while she was gathering flowers in the Vale of Nysa. In desolation, Demeter neglected the harvest, which led to famine. Zeus demanded that Hades release Persephone to her mother. Because Persephone had eaten pomegranate seeds in the underworld, it was agreed that she had to remain one-third of the year with Hades. This arrangement is said to account for the creation of the seasons.

MEANING: Contemplation Persephone was seemingly treated as something of a passive figure, bargained with and argued over by her patriarchal father, overprotective mother, and pitiless suitor, with her needs neglected and ignored. Ironically, she ended up with the best deal, spending part of her time in the underworld, giving her a chance to reflect and regenerate, while still permitted to return to her loved ones. Persephone's story reminds us to ignore the noise and demands of others. She guides you to spend some time in precious solitude. It's time to switch off, detach, and align with your inner needs. Find some alone time. Walk in nature and contemplate major decisions. It may be that you need to pour your resources and energies into inner self-improvement, such as therapy. This enhances relationship potential, as you become more content and authentic.

Retreat and breathe—
all will become clear.

X Tyche: The Wheel of Fortune

KEYWORDS: Decisive moments, fortune, lucky bolts from the blue

Tyche was the Greek goddess of fortune, chance, providence, and fate, sometimes also known as Eutykhia. It is said that she controlled the fortune and prosperity of a city, and is often seen wearing a mural crown, which resembled the walls of a city, and carrying a large horn of plenty to spread to others. She was said to have been one of Persephone's companions, although absent the day of her abduction. We owe the idea of flipping a coin to Tyche—in the time of Alexander the Great, it was Tyche's image on coins. If Tyche came up on the flip, the answer was likely to be lucky.

MEANING: Destiny Tyche's presence signifies amazing good fortune. There can be marvelous encounters and lucky breaks when she is present. Tyche is urging you to grab chances and run with them, and build on good things—and this will help bring more positivity and bounty into your life. Understand that luck is close, even if it doesn't feel that way. Tyche asks you to remember you can make your own good fortune too—your intuition is highly developed and it can lead you to opportunity. Wealth, in the form of promotions and pay rises, is possible, and Tyche is an excellent help with job hunting too. If you have your own business, you should find that success and prosperity are beckoning. Should you wish to move, this card suggests you may discover your dream home now. Love potentially blooms for singles.

I ride the waves of life.

XI Athena: Strength

KEYWORDS: Courage, confidence, precision

Athena is the famed Greek goddess of war and protectress of cities, and also rules handicraft. The daughter of Zeus, Athena is said to have been created without a mother, emerging fully grown from her father's forehead in complete battle gear, armed and ready to fight. Her birth triggered earthquakes and tidal waves. Athena is said to have had a complex relationship with her brother Ares, god of war, with sibling rivalry being an issue. While Ares had a blood lust and would act as a mercenary, fighting for any cause, Athena had a more ethical perspective. She would only use her prowess on the battlefield to fight for things she believed in and had merit. Her cerebral take on battle meant she was a superior fighter to her brother because she had clarity and could strategize.

MEANING: Power Athena's power and integrity are on your side. If there are obstacles to tackle, you have what is required to deal with them. Like Athena, you have stamina, might, and persistence, combined with intelligence and an ability to see the bigger picture; you understand that an iron fist in a velvet glove brings results. By using tactical strategies, as well as confidence and assertiveness, you can get what you want and protect those you love. Athena assures you that victory is close—and if it feels like you are going through hell, she is telling you to keep going. You have the strength to do so.

Strength from within is the greatest of all.

XII Dhumavati: The Hanged Man

KEYWORDS: Letting go, new perspectives, stasis

Known as "the Smoky One," the Indian goddess Dhumavati is a widow, the matron of the marginalized and of those who have regrets. Legend has it that she originated when Sati, the first wife of Lord Shiva—one of the most important gods in Hinduism—was hungry and left unfed. Sati was so famished that she devoured her husband. Once she had swallowed her husband, he was furious and asked to be let out. She did so—but Shiva still cursed her to undergo the pain of being a widow. Suddenly, smoke emitted from her body and enveloped her, and she became Dhumavati, the crone-like goddess. She separated from her husband and went on to live a hermit-like existence.

MEANING: Surrender Dhumavati's presence can indicate the need for patience, surrender, and faith. If only Sati had managed to hold in her hunger without acting rashly, she might have had a different fate. Perhaps you still have a chance to hit the pause button before acting too soon. Dhumavati also reminds us that life goes on, even if we do make a wrong move. This goddess is an expert in the art of survival. Request her assistance—she has hidden knowledge. She calls you to take a breath and understand what no longer serves you. Look at your world from a new perspective and see the openings that you hadn't spotted before. Wisdom can be found through experience. Business, money, or love matters appear to reach a standstill, but accept this and wait—change will come at the right time.

Stillness grants perspective.

XIII Ragana: Death

KEYWORDS: Beginnings, release, transformation

Hailing from Lithuania, Ragana is a goddess with psychic powers. She resides within the night and her name derives from the Lithuanian verb "redzet," meaning "to see." Ragana represents change and transformation—with her red wand, she has power over fertility and menopause. She is a goddess of death, but her powers can also miraculously heal and regenerate. She controls fertility and the milk supply of women and animals. Ragana is the guardian of nature's cycles: creation, growth, decline, and destruction. Our fear of the unknown and change can be seen in the world's treatment of Ragana. Originally venerated, she became feared as Christianity spread. The word "ragana" became synonymous with "witch." Ragana can transform into an animal or a beautiful young maiden (she is sometimes portrayed as a crone) who can devour men sexually. Men fear her—she has been described as "patriarchy's nightmare." However, Ragana has the power to make positive change—just as power is being reclaimed today by women everywhere.

MEANING: Endings You are stepping through the portal of transformation. One door is closing, but look—another one is open! Take strength from Ragana and step forward in power to a new reality. It is time to let go of what no longer serves you and embrace a potentially brilliant new beginning. This may feel like a jolt initially—perhaps something from beyond your own control has shaken everything up. Ragana is telling you, "You've got this. You have the power. Use it well." It's time to wave goodbye to the past. This may be difficult, but renewal is beckoning. What is meant to remain in your life will do so. But do not resist change as it will make the situation more difficult.

I'm willing to transform and rebuild my power.

XIV Bao Gu: Temperance

I heal the world with love and wisdom.

KEYWORDS: Balance, patience, purpose

Bao Gu was born a mortal, but has become a goddess and is venerated in China. She was a talented healer, raised and schooled in a monastery, where she learned magic, alchemy, and medical techniques, including acupuncture. She especially believed in the restorative effects of water. Her talents made her famed—it was unusual for a woman to be such a revered healer. Among her accomplishments was helping groups of villagers who were weak and tired, and had dark, yellow faces and swollen bodies. Using a treatment called moxibustion, acupuncture, and herbalism, she restored them to health. Bao Gu's mastery of alchemy was so complete that she never died but transformed into an immortal or fairy. It is believed that she ascended to heaven, so she is addressed respectfully as a goddess and female divinity.

MEANING: Healing Bao Gu brings healing to those around her. Her presence now is bringing you the gifts of restoration and equilibrium. Bao Gu may also be indicating that you are the person who is like a balm to others. In terms of answering a question or a conundrum, she suggests a response of moderation, balance, and patience. Make time and adjustments for your health and wellbeing. Put up boundaries to protect your mind and body if need be. If others are being tricky or unreasonable, take a deep breath and exhale calm, love, and healing. Pour oil on any troubled waters with a reasoned approach and things will get back on track.

XV Ananke: The Devil

KEYWORDS: Change, transformation, endings

The origins of Ananke, Greek goddess of destiny, are shrouded in mystery. Ananke is seen as the primordial mother, who emerged at the beginning of time, and is seen as the personification of fate and necessity. A serpentine being, her first act was to mate with her male counterpart, Kronos, and together they formed the world and became the ultimate power of the universe, controlling fate. Ananke and Kronos are said to encircle the cosmos to drive the rotation of the heavens and the eternal passage of time. They are beyond the reach of the younger gods, whose fates they are believed to control.

MEANING: Rebirth All-powerful Ananke is the goddess of whatever needs to happen—predestined fate that cannot be resisted. Her presence signifies that one major phase in your life is ending, and she is opening the door to a new reality. It's time to take a deep breath, say goodbye to what has been, and look your future in the eye. Do not try and battle with the force of change. Understand that it cannot be held back, but you can work with it. If you dig your heels in, fate will take control. It's time to wave goodbye to any attachments that are not serving you. As humans, we are forever growing and moving forward to learn. Whether it's in love, work, money, or life in general, you are leaving behind beliefs, attitudes, and behaviors that are past their sell-by date. In the future, you will develop healthier, stronger relationships and better strategies.

Be mistress of your own destiny.

XVI Pele: The Tower

KEYWORDS: Trauma, sudden change, freedom

Pele, a Hawaiian goddess in the form of a volcano, is certainly unpredictable. As the goddess of the element of Fire, Pele is also considered an "akua:" the sacred embodiment of a natural element. Legend has it that she was born in Tahiti, where her lustiness with her sister's husband got her into trouble, and she was banished and traveled in a canoe to Hawaii. Her furious sister, Namakaokahai, goddess of the sea, pursued Pele and beat her, leaving her for dead. Pele managed to escape to Oahu and the other islands, where she dug several giant fire pits, including the Halemaumau crater at the summit of Kilauea, one of the world's most active volcanoes. Namakaokahai pursued Pele and killed her—but Pele became a goddess and resides in the crater to this day.

MEANING: Upheaval "Expect the unexpected" is the message from Pele. Sudden change is on the horizon. It may not necessarily be scary. There are times we need ground-breaking transformation, and sudden and dramatic events are likely now. You may be saying goodbye to a job, a relationship, or an attitude that has underpinned your life in some way. The old ways have served their time, and you must find new ways of living and loving. To this day, Pele appears throughout the Hawaiian isles, shapeshifting in the form of women of all types, young, old, gorgeous, haggard. You are being granted the same ability—life is changing and it's time to transform.

Change can be for the better.

XVII Elpis: The Star

KEYWORDS: Fulfillment, purpose, renewal

Elpis is the personification of hope in Greek mythology. She is part of one of the best-known Greek myths. Zeus, the god of the sky, and the other gods created the first woman, Pandora. Each one of them gave her a gift. She was given beauty and charm and taught to be cunning, determined, and curious. Pandora was also given a jar (later known as a box) and was warned never to open it. Pandora's curiosity got the better of her and she released evils into the world. Realizing what she had done, she quickly closed it again. Elpis—hope—alone remained inside, the lid having been shut before she could escape.

MEANING: Hope Whatever is happening in your life, allow yourself a smile. Even if you feel you have made a mistake, hope and healing are with you. You should find yourself feeling very positive and serene, connected with spirit and looking toward new horizons. Elpis's presence is indicating that you can heal and look forward. It's time to have a spring in your step. There will be renewal and joy in relationships, money will start to flow again, and you will see the flicker of opportunity, which motivates and invigorates you. Artistic endeavors are well starred now, and if you wish to have a job in the healing sector, you are being guided that this is the right thing to do.

I have faith in my dreams.

XVIII Selene: The Moon

Even in the mists, my intuition lights the way, one step at a time.

KEYWORDS: Mystery, dreams, inner guidance

The silvery moon is a symbol of femininity and mystery, and Greek goddess Selene is the personification of this. Selene bathes in the ocean before riding up to the sky in her chariot every night, pulled by silver horses. Just as the full moon shines on us, Selene beams light on conundrums and mysteries, like female intuition, and is said to have the power to grant sleep. Selene's lovers include Pan and Zeus, with whom she had several children. Her most famous love affair was with the young shepherd Endymion, the male sleeping beauty. Some legends say Selene placed him under an eternal sleep spell so her lover could remain unchanged forever; others say it was Zeus who cast the misfortunate shepherd into eternal sleep in a cave on Mount Latmus. Selene visited Endymion and became the mother of 50 daughters.

MEANING: Illusion Sometimes the moon is visible, at other times she disappears. However, she is always there. This is the message that is being bestowed by Selene. You feel like your inner knowledge has left you. But take heart and know it is present. There may be something in your life that is not as it seems, or perhaps your judgment is being distorted by emotional distress or long-buried memories. Selene is asking you to process the hurt. Try guided meditation, Shamanic healing, or hypnosis. It's about bypassing the rigid, structured part of your brain and accessing pure intuition. Something in your current situation isn't quite as it's being presented—there is more to it than the facts being presented to you. When making big decisions, don't take things at face value. Dreams, intuition, and inner guidance are your friends now. Selene is telling you to go deep—and sleep on it. Then all will be clear.

XIX Magec: The Sun

KEYWORDS: Success, vitality, love

One of the principal divinities of the Guanche people, the Indigenous people of the Canary Islands in the Atlantic Ocean, Magec is also known as the god of the sun and light. Magec is notable as a non-binary deity. According to legend, Guayota, the devil, imprisoned Magec within Tenerife's Mount Teide, sucking the light out of the world. The Guanches petitioned Archaman, the supreme god, for the return of Magec. After a battle, Archaman freed Magec and sealed Guayota back in the volcano. Light returned. It's believed any eruption of the volcano is Guayota trying to escape. The Guanches have a tradition of lighting bonfires during the time of eruptions to scare Guayota and keep him within the volcano.

MEANING: Joy Here comes the sunshine after a period of darkness! You can expect a boost in wellbeing and mood. If you've been waiting for matters to get better, start smiling! After some challenges, you are stepping into success, and are full of energy and a zest for life. You're exuding confidence and, following the law of attraction, abundance is coming your way. Family life is blessed, and if you are planning to extend your brood, there could be good news for you. If you've had a disagreement with someone, reconciliations can happen now. Celebrations and vacations are beautifully starred by this card. Love and proposals are also possibilities.

I shine my light and my radiance attracts more success.

XX Rhiannon: Judgment

KEYWORDS: Second chances, reflection, forgiveness

According to Celtic legend, Rhiannon, the radiant goddess of inner truth, was first spied by King Pwyll, as she was wearing gold and majestically rode a beautiful white horse. Their destiny was to be wed. However, Rhiannon didn't fall pregnant, and gossip abounded that she was a sorceress. Finally, Rhiannon gave birth to a son, Pryderi. Unfortunately, servants meant to be watching over the newborn fell asleep and the baby disappeared. The servants blamed Rhiannon and said she'd eaten her own child. Pwyll ordered Rhiannon to spend seven years seated near the horseblock by his gate, retelling her story to all who approached, and then carrying them to court on her back like a horse. She bore her punishment and lived in hope. Many years later, Pryderi was returned to his parents by a lord who had rescued him from a monster and raised the baby as his own son. Rhiannon was redeemed.

MEANING: Inner calling Rhiannon's story reminds us that the truth can set us free—and that healing and second chances do happen. You can discover spirituality and the best you. You are being offered another opportunity. Trust your own innate sense of what is right and wrong. Whatever hurt has been piled on, you're at a crossroads, and need to make a choice—a judgment, even. What have past life lessons taught you? It's time for wounds to be healed and for salvation. Forgiveness is a big theme of this card. Take a breath, reach out to others, and reassess the past. Use your inner judgment to work out what situations to leave behind forever, and which deserve your time, energy, and love.

The daily choices I make now align me with my life's purpose.

XXI Lakshmi: The World

KEYWORDS: Fulfillment, possibilities, successful conclusions

Lakshmi, lady of wealth, good fortune, and beauty is one of the most beloved goddesses in India and is married to Vishnu, the principal Hindu deity. Lakshmi bestows abundance, luxury, and happiness. Commonly portrayed as a beautiful woman with four arms, she stands on a lotus flower, usually flanked by elephants. Lakshmi brings good fortune to all to whom she turns her attention. She aided Indra, the warrior god, in his fight against the demons, but one day, Indra arrogantly tossed a garland of sacred flowers to the floor. Lakshmi was angered by his attitude and fled to the Milky Ocean, taking with her success and fortune, and leaving demons in control. Vishnu told Indra that the gods would need to churn the Milky Ocean to regain Lakshmi and her blessings. After a thousand years of churning, Lakshmi reappeared as a beautiful woman standing on a lotus flower and helped to save the world from demons.

MEANING: Achievement This story of Lakshmi highlights successful conclusions and reminds us that good fortune is possible with hard work and a little humility. A long-term project, relationship, or career matter has come full circle and is reaching fruition. This may be an engagement, a birth, a promotion, or another kind of career goal that has been, or is about to be, reached. Travel may also be a part of your immediate future. This card represents achievement and satisfaction. You feel whole and complete and you're enjoying your sense of accomplishment. Celebrate! Things are turning out how you wish. Yes, you have learned lessons on the way, but you have also enjoyed some good fortune. Remember to be thankful and take a moment to see how far you have come.

Victory is mine.

The Minor Arcana

The Major Arcana cards encapsulate big turning points and significant situations in your life. The Minor Arcana cards address the more everyday events we experience. To understand the Minor Arcana, you can use the guide below. As you become more accustomed to your cards, you will notice recurring themes, so jot down your findings in a notebook.

The Four Suits
The four suits in the Minor Arcana are: Wands, Cups, Swords, and Pentacles. Each suit has 14 cards (ten numbered cards and a King, Queen, Knight, and Page). The four suits each represent a different area of your life:

Wands
Action, initiative, invention, travel, growth, energy
Swords
Intellect, challenges, conflict, mind, decisions
Pentacles
Work, money, home, long-term goals, family, health
Cups
Emotions, intuition, love, feelings, relationships

The Elements
Gods and goddesses' connection to the concept of the elements is evident in many ancient and magical traditions across the world. In ancient Greek philosophy, the universe is said to comprise four elements: Fire, Air, Earth, and Water. The four elements are usually arranged as four corners, but can also be arranged with Fire at the top (think the sun), then Air, followed by Earth and then Water. Each possesses its own "energy" and symbolic meaning. None is wholly good or bad; indeed each brings its own positive and negative side. Each tarot suit in this deck is connected to a particular element.

FIRE: Passionate, hot, potentially dangerous, but also warm-hearted and energy-bringing. The suit of Wands is connected to the element of Fire: Temperamental, volatile, and full of energy. These qualities are characterized by the Aztec goddess of fire and hearth. She is associated with health, fertility, wealth, and abundance. Mixcoatl was the Aztec god of the hunt who gave fire to humanity. He was also associated with the stars, particularly with the starry band known as the Milky Way.

AIR: Air brings movement and communication. The Air element relates to knowledge, action, power, and change. It can be a gentle breeze, or a hurricane. The suit of Swords is connected to this element. It signifies action, ambition, courage, change, and conflict. We need this energy to help us get to where we need to be. In Hawaiian mythology, the goddess of wind, Hine-Tu-Whenua, aids sailors to reach their destinations safely, and La'a Maomao, the god of wind, is fabled to have been created in the midst of chaos, but can grant forgiveness and understanding.

EARTH: From the ground beneath our feet to the food we put in our mouths, this element is concrete and tangible. Grounded, stable, supportive, and fertile, it's associated with the material side of life. In tarot, the Earth element is represented by the suit of Pentacles, and has connections with nature, body, wealth, the material world, and stability. In African mythology, Ala formed the earth and is the source of life. She is the mother goddess of the earth. Her father, Chuku, is also an earth deity, the Supreme Creator, originator of spirits, people, animals, and all that lives and has sacred association with trees.

WATER: The key to life, water refreshes and cleanses us, but its power can be forceful, even fatal. It's feminine, fluid, and can change form as if by magic. In the tarot, water relates to the suit of Cups. This element connects with emotions, feelings, dreams, psychic insight, and empathy. In Greek mythology, Dione, water goddess of fertility and divination, was known for predictions and prophesies. Meanwhile, Oceanus, god of the great earth-encircling River Ocean, is the boundary and threshold between our world and whatever is beyond.

The Numbered Cards

Each number in the Minor Arcana has an association which gives you more information on how to interpret it. By putting the numbers together with the suits, you can get more insight into predictions and meanings.

Aces (1, I): Beginnings, initiative, drive, potential, and new opportunities
Twos (2, II): Balance and partnerships, also dilemmas
Threes (3, III): Interactions, teamwork, and communications
Fours (4, IV): Rest, stability, contemplation
Fives (5, V): Conflict, challenges, obstacles
Sixes (6, VI): Growth, overcoming challenges, clarity
Sevens (7, VII): Faith, potential, confidence, determination, and patience
Eights (8, VIII): Progress, reward, change
Nines (9, IX): Heightened energy, fruition
Tens (10, X): Outcomes, completions, rewards and consequences

The Court Cards

The Court Cards can symbolize people in our lives or individuals we will soon meet, as well as representing influences. The Page cards, for example, can stand for youthful people, but also denote new phases and beginnings. Knights can indicate figures in our lives who are vigorous, brave, and reflect periods of activity and action. Queen cards embody wise, experienced figures in your life and are indicators of power, potential, and advice. The Kings can signify authority and power in the form of both people and situations. They also point to drive and ambition.

36 The Minor Arcana

Ace of Wands

KEYWORDS: Breakthrough, growth, spark

MEANING: **Creativity** The Ace of Wands is telling you, "Just go for it!" Say YES to opportunity. This isn't a slam dunk guarantee of success—you'll have to put the work in. However, it is a very positive indication that you have all the abilities and talents to get what you want. This is a fantastic card for new work and creative ventures, and a wonderfully positive indication for pregnancy and fledgling relationships. Travel is also brilliantly forecast here. Don't be surprised if you get a chance to fly off somewhere or even live overseas—and there could be a romantic twist. Time to step forward with a spring in your step!

Two of Wands

KEYWORDS: Progress, partnership, discovery

MEANING: **Self-worth** The Two of Wands is telling you that it's time for the work to start. It's time to formulate a clear plan of action and manifest your heart's desire. Partnerships are especially well starred, so whether it's pairing up with someone in friendship, business, creativity, or a relationship, things should be fruitful and positive. Existing dynamic duos will also enjoy positivity, expansion, and growth. A romance that is kindled in the workplace could be rather wonderful for singles. This card may also be a sign that a decision needs to be made in love or career, whether it's a choice of jobs or suitors. Which one should you pick? The one that brings you joy.

Three of Wands

KEYWORDS: Expansion, foresight, celebration

MEANING: **Travel** The Three of Wands is telling you to unleash your desire to run free—it represents freedom, adventure, travel, moving abroad, and foreign lands. In love, you could be looking at heart-stopping romance, proposals, elopements, and enticing encounters in far-flung destinations—which could lead to a permanent bond. Work projects and business ventures should blossom, and you'll be delighted. For those in creative fields who have been waiting for that moment of recognition, this is a brilliant card. Hard work and application pay off. This card is not about dumb luck, but signifies foresight and forward planning. Feel confident and believe in yourself. The goddesses favor the brave.

Four of Wands

KEYWORDS: New friends, stability, trust

MEANING: **Celebrations** The Four of Wands is a joyous card of celebration, coming together with loved ones, and making new friends. It signifies a harmonious, happy, and loving home environment. You can build stability now—and it's a great time to enjoy the company of others, whether it's to mark a milestone or just get together for good times. This card can represent parties and reunions, vacations, honeymoons, and housewarming parties. It also may represent the reaching of a particularly important goal—think job interviews, exams, or a promotion. There's a good chance you can raise a glass or two of something fizzy and feel proud!

Five of Wands

KEYWORDS: Change, ego, frustration

MEANING: **Conflict** The Five of Wands is all about conflict and disagreement and how these elements can cause stir in your life. The status quo cannot survive, and you are at loggerheads with someone or something. Tensions and battles abound. The situation requires resolution. Unfortunately, everyone wants to have their say, which just leads to a lot of noise. If you work in a competitive field such as journalism, fashion, or sport, you could find you have to pit yourself against a competitor. Or you may find yourself having to deal with a love rival. Whatever the situation, you are being reminded to rise above the noise, stick to the facts, and be constructive.

Six of Wands

KEYWORDS: Empowerment, confidence, recognition

MEANING: **Triumph** Getting the Six of Wands is very positive. Victory is beckoning! You have reached a point indicating that success is near, or perhaps are receiving a notification that you are at some kind of milestone near your ultimate destination. It's a yes card, so if you are waiting to find out whether you have passed a test or are going to prevail in a dispute, you should be very pleased. Honors and endorsements can all occur now, and promotions and business growth look very likely. There may be some way to go, but all things are going as they should, and a happy outcome looks likely.

Seven of Wands

KEYWORDS: Defense, challenges, trust

MEANING: **Protectiveness** The Seven of Wands means you need to defend your corner. You have something precious that is worth protecting—whether it's an idea, a relationship, or your own self-esteem. Someone is picking a fight and you need to maintain your boundaries without being reduced to their level while still retaining your sense of self-worth. Reject overly aggressive overtures and psychodramas and remain cool and collected. Other people have their own issues and may become territorial or irrational. Legal battles and divorce could be a factor now, or you might be in a profession such as the law where you need to battle it out. Remain strong, and with a clear purpose, and you will overcome.

Eight of Wands

KEYWORDS: Communication, action, travel

MEANING: **Movement** The Eight of Wands is all about putting your best foot forward and conveying your thoughts to others. You are entering a very positive and fast-paced period of activity when everyone will be interested to hear your point of view. Make the most of this time to manifest your goals and dreams. It should be good news if you're going for job interviews or putting proposals to supportive and influential individuals. Home-moving delays should be resolved. Amid this whirl of activity, love could very well pop up. Those interested in romance can achieve success online or traveling. Listen to messages that come through now—they may be bringing opportunity.

Nine of Wands

KEYWORDS: Resilience, challenges, empowerment

MEANING: **Persistence** The Nine of Wands embodies the energy of when you are so close—yet so far—from reaching success. One more push is needed, yet you feel exhausted and challenged. This card is encouraging you to "keep going," like a cheering passer-by to a marathon runner on his last legs. The battle has almost been won. It is also pointing out that there may be irritations and a few more minor trials to get through before you reach your goal. Someone may come into your life who will transform your efforts. You may have to step out of your comfort zone at least once more to reach success. But see this as a sign of hope and encouragement that you will make it.

Ten of Wands

KEYWORDS: Emotional freedom, completion, closure

MEANING: **Burdens of responsibility** The Ten of Wands reflects a period when you feel put upon. It's as if the universe has loaded you with one too many responsibilities or jobs, and you are left saying, "Hold on!" Remember, this is a temporary state of affairs. It may be time to think about prioritization; you may even come to a realization that the cost you are being asked to bear is too great. For example, you may find that work is impinging on your social life or family responsibilities. Or you may realize that getting to where you want to be will result in taking on more responsibility. It could be time to re-evaluate. Only you know what is best for you. Either way, this card is telling you that the end is in sight.

Page of Wands

KEYWORDS: Playfulness, fresh ideas, apprehension

MEANING: Adventure The Page of Wands signifies passion to succeed, but also inexperience and nervousness of the unknown and what is to come. You're just going for it—starting out on a new journey or project without much of a plan and seeing where it takes you. Career changes may even occur. The start of a flirty and freewheeling romance could be coming up. It might not lead to life-long commitment, but just enjoy! It may be that a younger person has a crush on you, and you can't help but be flattered. Alternatively, this may signify the rekindling of an old flame from your younger days. Friendships are also looking bright on the horizon. Artists, free spirits, or vital sporty types may be entering your life.

Knight of Wands

KEYWORDS: Courage, energy, charm

MEANING: Free spirit The Knight of Wands is symbolic of a wish not to be held down or bound by convention. Naturally rebellious, thrilling, and fun to be around, this knight ushers excitement into your life. Be brave, take a chance! Expect the pace of your life to zoom ahead. Socially, expect a bit of a whirl as you land up at glam parties and unexpected social events. This could be the best time to get away and travel. In career and work, it's all about getting things done. Fantastic career moves and jobs abroad could happen now. An out-of-the-blue event might happen soon. Expect the unexpected.

Queen of Wands

KEYWORDS: Confidence, independence, determination

MEANING: **Passion** The Queen of Wands is all about throwing your soul into something, truly owning your projects, and being warm and passionate, firstly to those you care about, but also to the world at large. Confident and fiery, this queen urges you to live life to the full. Meet people, make connections, and love with all your heart. This could be a real person in your life, someone who wants the best for you and is like a cheerleader. If you're looking to get pregnant, this card brings positive news, but exciting trips, passion projects, and a jam-packed diary are also possibilities.

King of Wands

KEYWORDS: Dominance, entrepreneurial spirit, honesty

MEANING: **Leader** The King of Wands has a fiery feel—a bold and fearless type who is willing to stand up for his beliefs and is not one to follow the crowd. This may well be someone you recognize in your life. However, this card can also indicate that you will step into a role like this. You'll have a clear vision and others will be drawn to you. Clear-eyed and charismatic, you can be an inspiration to others. You know your mind and can push forward with purpose. In real terms, this means following your dreams and doing what is on your mind, even if you—or others—fear it could be reckless. Make a move on that person you have a crush on, or quit your job and start your own business.

Ace of Swords

KEYWORDS: Structure, concentration, victory

MEANING: **Breakthrough** The Ace of Swords is telling you: "Now is the moment!" You're about to experience a breakthrough. Perhaps you have not been told the whole story, and something comes along that cuts through all the fogginess. You are viewing a situation with fresh clarity, which will lead to greater certainty and action. This can mean writing that book or making the move you've always planned. It could be letting someone know you like them and striking up a new friendship. You will also look at certain relationships in a new light. Sometimes it means cutting ties with someone who is no longer offering you positivity.

Two of Swords

KEYWORDS: Uncertainty, pathways, stalemate

MEANING: **Difficult choices** The Two of Swords symbolizes the times when we are forced to make a choice—and it's not an easy one. Neither option seems ideal. But unless we move past this stalemate, there can be no more progress. Whether it's in work, love, or friendship, you know something has to change but are caught between a rock and a hard place. It may be that someone else is involved, which complicates matters. You cannot stick your head in the sand. Prolonging the agony won't help. Be honest. You know what to do. Take action, then you can move forward to live and love in a better way.

Three of Swords

KEYWORDS: Separation, upset, loss

MEANING: **Heartbreak** The Three of Swords is a card that signifies loss. This may be a tough message to receive. On the other hand, you are being given a valuable opportunity to prepare for the experience. You can take a philosophical approach and remember that loss is part of life. This can signify the ending of a relationship, job, or friendship. You may even have to endure personal betrayal. You might also have to relinquish a belief, which could prove painful. The grief may sting but focus on the future. The truth is, you do have control over how you handle this episode and your future. This situation may be coming to a close, but you have so much else to live for.

Four of Swords

KEYWORDS: Peace, sanctuary, recovery

MEANING: **Recuperation** The Four of Swords is a moment of rest. It seems like you may have been overdoing things. You have endured certain obstacles and losses, but now it is time to retreat and rejuvenate. You will be ready to go forth into the world soon enough. Perhaps you have been licking your wounds after a romance or relationship strife, or maybe work has been pushing you to your limit. You must take the time to pause and surrender to rest and relaxation. Of course, there may be new challenges to come—that's life, after all. But now it's time for nurture. Be kind to yourself. You'll come out stronger than before.

Five of Swords

KEYWORDS: Disputes, aggression, stress

MEANING: **Conflict** The Five of Swords reveals bad blood. There has been a row or a disagreement and a falling out. Even if you feel like you have the moral high ground, you may not feel you have won. The cost of going head to head with another is often very great. If you are involved in an ongoing conflict, this card asks, "is it worth it?" There are times when you really do need to fight your corner, but it's time to weigh up matters. Are you really 100 percent in the right? And even if you are, if the fighting is causing you heartache, is it time to concede? Ideally, rise above pettiness and complications. Cut your losses and move on.

Six of Swords

KEYWORDS: Regeneration, travel, new destinations

MEANING: **Healing** The Six of Swords is all about moving into calmer waters. You've had to endure hardships and angst aplenty, but fear not—better times are on the horizon. What happens next is a healing balm; life is going to be less of a struggle and more of a smooth ride. Trust your intuition now. It's time to protect yourself and show a bit of self-care. Escaping to a spa or overseas destination will feel enticing. This card symbolizes the kind of vacation where you relax and enjoy life, or a trip across water. In relationships this is all about healing the hurt and getting back to a healthy equilibrium. For career, you may be enjoying new chances, perhaps away from home, where you can reinvigorate.

Seven of Swords

KEYWORDS: Deception, victimization, loss

MEANING: Betrayal The Seven of Swords is telling you that there is some kind of deception going on. Perhaps you are the victim of someone trying to deceive you, or not telling you the whole truth. Perhaps a friend or lover is not quite what they seem on first appearance. Maybe a relative is getting into your business. Or perhaps you are the one trying to get away with something. Depending on the situation, you need to get in touch with your intuition or inner moral compass. In certain situations, this is a reminder to be strategic and a little bit canny in your dealings with others. You may need to look for clever hacks or shortcuts. It could be that you are trying to escape from a situation that is no longer right for you.

Eight of Swords

KEYWORDS: Powerlessness, feeling trapped, possibilities

MEANING: Restriction On the surface, the Eight of Swords can feel like a tough card to receive. It alludes to feeling trapped and wishing to escape. A feeling of powerlessness is making you feel frustrated. Whether it's a relationship or job that has passed its expiration date, circumstances are conspiring to make you feel you're in a room without a door. However, like the escape room games, there is a way out. The feeling of being imprisoned is mainly psychological. Look at the situation from another angle or perspective. There are, in fact, some eye-opening possibilities. Tap into your inner power and ingenuity and you will discover them.

The Suit of Swords AIR

Nine of Swords

KEYWORDS: Mindset, worry, fear

MEANING: Anxiety The Nine of Swords is that feeling when you wake up at 3 am and a worry grips your soul—you get caught in a vicious circle of negativity. It may be that you are carrying concerns about a loved one's wellbeing, and this is weighing heavily. However, the irony is that whatever your thoughts are telling you, your greatest enemy is your own bleak mindset. Your obsessive thoughts are getting out of hand, and you are getting in your own way. So if you're fretting about losing your job, or your lover leaving you, it's time to switch to a more positive mode—this card is a warning that downward-spiraling thoughts may manifest what you fear. The good news is that you have the power to create a positive reality.

Ten of Swords

KEYWORDS: Transition, loss, release

MEANING: Growth The Ten of Swords is about endings, which will in turn lead to new beginnings. There's no doubt that there will be an ending. A relationship may break up. A friend could walk out of your life. Your worldview may be shattered, and you will look at things in a very different way. The message from this card is: Remember, you cannot control everything. Some matters are beyond our control. Let go and accept what is happening. The only thing you can control is your reaction to external events. You are discovering just how strong and resilient your spirit is. Like a phoenix, you will rise again.

Page of Swords

KEYWORDS: Curiosity, thirst for knowledge, determination

MEANING: **Awareness** The Page of Swords encourages you to keep sharp. You could be very excited by a new project or person in your life and wish to get going on making things happen. And although there is a thrill in the air, this card sounds a note of caution. It's possible a certain someone around you has their own agenda. See this as an exploration, rather than the definitive road to travel down. You may be prone to making errors along the way, but you can learn from your mistakes. Communicating your ideas is very much an aspect of this card. Think vlogs, social media, or podcasts—just don't forget attention to detail!

Knight of Swords

KEYWORDS: Drive, immaturity, fickleness

MEANING: **Action-oriented** The Knight of Swords is a force of nature—the kind who crashes into a situation and causes mayhem. In a reading this could represent your current state of mind, showing how you are pushing ahead in a situation—and to hell with the consequences. It could also refer to another person's actions and personality. There could be heated discussions and spats; there may be some upsets and eye-opening incidents along the way. With love and family there may be tensions that leave you confused. Be aware that by going in headlong, you might rush in unaware of potential challenges.

Queen of Swords

KEYWORDS: Independence, balance, objectivity

MEANING: Dispassionate The Queen of Swords has a sternness and a strength. This lady is not for bending, although she is fair and impartial. There is also a warm heart beneath her imperious exterior. This card may be advising you to take inspiration from her dignified strength in a tricky situation, especially if you feel like your compassionate nature is being exploited. Or perhaps in a reading it refers to someone in your life who embodies these characteristics and who can inspire and guide you. You're being advised that standing up and putting boundaries in place can be a positive thing for all concerned.

King of Swords

KEYWORDS: Structure, direction, stubbornness

MEANING: Tenacity The King of Swords is about head over heart, using logic and brain power, and behaving in a methodical fashion. This individual may want the best for those in his domain, and be loyal, but he can come across as emotionally removed and cold in his dealings. This card could be advising you to adopt such a stance in dealing with a tricky situation, or he may denote an authoritative type in your life—a parent or boss. When it comes to love, look out for romances with those in authority—doctors, lawyers, or military types. This card may be saying that you need to let your head rule in affairs of the heart.

Ace of Pentacles

KEYWORDS: Financial opportunities, affluence, growth

MEANING: **New beginning** Goddess energy is granting you a brilliant new beginning with the Ace of Pentacles! A new door is opening and there are likely to be some positive events relating to work and money. You should feel optimistic and inspired in the midst of this exciting energy. Abundance is coming your way in the form of security and stability. This could be the time to make your dreams a reality, so start manifesting new jobs, businesses investments, and abundance. Expect loans and house deals to be given the seal of approval. Relationships are also blessed and likely to flourish in wonderful ways.

Two of Pentacles

KEYWORDS: Flexibility, choices, variety

MEANING: **Balancing resources** The universe is presenting you with a dilemma with the Two of Pentacles. It seems you are juggling something or trying to make a decision. This could concern a job, a house move, or a career decision. The goddess's message is: "Life is calling on you to be versatile." It might feel like you need to reassess how to balance different priorities. This could be related to finances, but also to your own energies. It's important to see the big picture and avoid getting caught up in day-to-day demands. Try to think about ways you can better manage your time, assets, and priorities. Keep an eye on your bank balance as there may be an unforeseen expense. Make sure there is a rainy-day fund!

Three of Pentacles

KEYWORDS: Studying, achievement, focus

MEANING: Learning The Three of Pentacles denotes accomplishment; it indicates the completion of a goal. Heading toward successful achievement and the joy of working together with others are all celebrated here. You are looking toward success. There is a need to recognize that you don't know everything yet, or have full access to all the facts, so avoid arrogance or over-confidence. Take on board new knowledge and skills. Hard work, determination, dedication, and commitment will be your tickets to success. If you have poured your energies and talents into a project, you should feel satisfied and enjoy the recognition and plaudits coming your way.

Four of Pentacles

KEYWORDS: Money, prosperity, success

MEANING: Copiousness The Four of Pentacles indicates that money is certainly on your mind at the moment. Times may have been tough—but prosperity is not too far away now. You're also being asked questions by the universe as regards your attitude to money. Are you coining it in for good reason? Are you investing your money wisely? Are you getting to enjoy your wealth? It could be a matter of balance. Yes, you should save, but you also need to enjoy your money. It's time to reassess your attitude and ensure it's serving your interests in the best way possible. The good news is that if you can settle any disagreements with others over assets and investments, this could result in greater abundance.

Five of Pentacles

KEYWORDS: Money concern, fear, adversity

MEANING: Loss The Five of Pentacles suggests that there could be some unforeseen expense or loss coming up. It might not necessarily happen, but the card can be saying that a particular course of action might result in financial loss, so you should take care. There may be setbacks, loss of assets, or unexpected expenses. Remember: it will pass and you will overcome. It's vital to remember that your ability to create abundance can be sabotaged by a poverty of spirit. Don't forget to express your gratitude for small things and count your blessings to encourage a growth mindset.

Six of Pentacles

KEYWORDS: Charity, goodwill, gratitude

MEANING: Generosity Kindness and generosity are represented by the Six of Pentacles, especially if you have endured difficulties. It means the beginning of a period when you not only have plenty for yourself, but can offer help to others. Sharing and caring are highlighted as we offer our time and resources to others. This card could also represent somebody in your life who is very generous, as well as symbolizing your role in giving to and helping others. It's a positive card that represents a strong sense of community, signifying equality and fairness. It also reminds you that if you have been lucky, you should share your good fortune.

Seven of Pentacles

KEYWORDS: Results, growth, perseverance

MEANING: **Rewards** The Seven of Pentacles indicates that you've been working hard, and it's paying off. This card suggests you've put a lot of effort, grit, and determination into whatever you want to achieve. You understand the value of putting in time and energy now for longer-term rewards. This is reaffirming your vision and helping to show that you're on the right path. There may be obstacles, but just because something is difficult that doesn't mean you should give up. If you feel like a failure, it reminds you to look at the bigger picture and assess how far you have come. It may be that you need to take some time and reassess. But do not give up. One more push and you will get there.

Eight of Pentacles

KEYWORDS: Talent, high standards, mastery

MEANING: **Attainment** The Eight of Pentacles reveals that you are successfully applying the lessons of the past to your present situation. You are successful and skilled, and other people are noticing what you have to offer. This is a great card to get in relation to further education or study, or if you are honing your skills in an industry. You are becoming more professional and expert in a field. More broadly, you're becoming adept at the finer details of life, constantly improving and refining. Keep on going: it will lead to success. This is a great sign for good outcomes in interviews and exams, or turning a passion into a business.

Nine of Pentacles

KEYWORDS: Independence, self-sufficiency, home life

MEANING: **Prosperity** Congratulations: The Nine of Pentacles is signaling that you are now so close to achievement. Recognition of your abilities and efforts is on its way. Projects that you may have started a long time ago are beginning to yield the rewards you have craved. Enjoy this time. After the struggles, success seems even sweeter. Financial independence, wealth, and luxury are possible now, so treat yourself. Home improvements and sheer appreciation of the love and company of your family are also highlighted. At last, you are enjoying security and are thankful for that. It's a time when you can enjoy a sense of achievement and move forward.

Ten of Pentacles

KEYWORDS: Financial security, love, long-term success

MEANING: **Completion** The Ten of Pentacles indicates wonderful positivity—love, luck, and happiness. Once you have material stability, achieving contentment becomes a lot easier. Joint finances and investment decisions are highlighted. Happiness and security are yours. You have reached a point of completion and accomplishment in your journey. Successful career moves, canny financial investments, and blissful home life are all indicated, as are generous gifts. Making a commitment by moving in or marrying are possibilities; this includes the uniting of two families. It's about coming together with others and counting blessings. Inheritance, windfalls, and property purchases can happen now.

Page of Pentacles

KEYWORDS: Studiousness, grounding, determination

MEANING: Loyalty The Page of Pentacles is a beacon of good news and positivity. As with all the Court Cards, this may represent a person in your life who is ambitious and focused but also ethical and loyal. In terms of the energies the Page signifies, it's all about determination, focus, and perseverance. It may seem there's a lot to get through, but there is no need to feel overwhelmed. All the help and assistance is there—you just need to ask. Education, learning new skills, and pursuing fresh career paths are all wonderfully starred. There is good news on jobs, house sales, and money—relationships can be renewed too.

Knight of Pentacles

KEYWORDS: Practicality, hard work, commitment

MEANING: Manifestation The Knight of Pentacles indicates both fulfillment and overcoming difficulties. As an individual he is stoic, reliable, and helpful. As an energy, this is a time of responsibility and hard work that will by rights lead to the successful conclusion of a project. It urges you to keep doing what you've been doing. Tried and true methods are favored. Now is not the time to strike out in an entirely new direction. There is a recognition of responsibility. Slow and steady can win the day. You can achieve that promotion or relationship, but these things may require a little more time before manifesting. Think hard work, responsibility, and continued perseverance.

Queen of Pentacles

KEYWORDS: Generosity, caring, luxury

MEANING: **Unifying** The presence of the Queen of Pentacles is like a warm, maternal embrace. She may represent a female family member, mentor, or friend who has your best interests at heart. This is a time of equilibrium in your life and of prosperity and security. This can indicate healing in a very positive sense. There is growth in business, money, and love. You can achieve success by joining forces with others. It's possible that this Queen represents a business partner who can expand your world, or a new love interest who will improve your life. Pregnancies, marriage, and moves to the country are ripe possibilities now.

King of Pentacles

KEYWORDS: Security, discipline, abundance

MEANING: **Wisdom** The King of Pentacles embodies economic power—a pinnacle of ambition. He can represent an older male, a man with financial clout, power, and the ability to lead and aid you. This card may be predicting that you will meet someone like this in your love life. In terms of energy, this is all about strength and feeling confident—you are being assured you can handle your life. However, remember that you're not superhuman, so avoid taking on too much. This card represents high social status, principles, and being resourceful and energetic. Promotions, house purchases, and a boost to your pay packet are all potentials now.

Ace of Cups

KEYWORDS: New feelings, inventiveness, openness

MEANING: Tenderness The presence of the Ace of Cups is a wonderful message that should lift our hearts. There is a fresh start promised. New beginnings are heralded, especially in love and happiness. You are entering a period when new friendships can flourish, so open your heart to different people as it could be the start of something beautiful. Engagements and weddings could happen now. Amazing things are being sparked, and attending social events and parties can be the conduit. Creativity is also radiating now. Projects such as writing a book or starting a business based on your talents or childhood dreams can now soar.

Two of Cups

KEYWORDS: Love, partnership, mutual attraction

MEANING: Fulfillment The Two of Cups card means you should be rejoicing in love. It's about two becoming one, creating connections and unity. If you are in the early stage of a relationship, you should rejoice. This has the potential to grow into something rather wonderful. If you are single, keep alert—a soulmate could be arriving very soon. In relationships, you should nurture mutual respect and appreciation. Your partnership has the ability to develop into something remarkable. Together, you are more than two individuals. It's a sign of old flames being rekindled. In business, it indicates that partnerships can flourish.

Three of Cups

KEYWORDS: Community, gatherings, celebrations

MEANING: Friendship The Three of Cups represents happy times, friends, and coming together in celebration. Indeed, this card can predict an actual event, such as a happy reunion with friends or a celebration. In the broader sense, it's about delighting in the company of those whom we truly value and who make us smile. It's a wonderful indication of love—there could be a relationship coming into your life—perhaps sparked at a celebratory occasion or through mutual friends. If you're in a relationship, a milestone, anniversary, or some other way to honor your partnership may be on its way. Promotions and pregnancies are also possibilities.

Four of Cups

KEYWORDS: Contemplation, motivation, deliberation

MEANING: Meditation The Four of Cups reflects a feeling of restlessness. It's as if you're searching for something and seeking fulfillment; you just haven't found it yet. You know that you need to be in a better position before whatever happens next. This disillusionment may be a result of past disappointments. Accepting this and moving forward is a fantastic step to true contentment. Give yourself some time and space to inwardly reflect and understand what your heart truly desires. Why are you dissatisfied? Work that out—and then look up. Blessings are all around you!

Five of Cups

KEYWORDS: Loss, sadness, reflection

MEANING: **Disappointment** The Five of Cups reflects disappointment. Perhaps you are feeling disillusioned about a certain situation. This is about perception and feeling rather than material loss. A situation hasn't really turned out the way you hoped. You are wallowing in feelings of self-pity and regret. Letting go of things can be tough and it's easy to get stuck. The card indicates that you're digging your heels in but suggests it's time to learn and move on. This card may represent heartache but its message is that you can and should move on. Honor your experience—and then look toward the future.

Six of Cups

KEYWORDS: Healing, comfort, family

MEANING: **Nostalgia** The Six of Cups takes you down memory lane in a wonderful way. It's all about happy times from your past entering your present and making you smile. Reconnections with joyful childhood memories and old friends are possible. Finding your inner child and play will leave you feeling renewed and refreshed. You could meet up with first loves and old flames, reminiscing about the good times. In terms of love, this can indicate rekindling of romance. Rediscovering creativity can lead to amazing things. Children can come into your life too, opening up new additions and bringing happiness.

Seven of Cups

KEYWORDS: Choices, opportunities, confusion

MEANING: Abundance of options The Seven of Cups card represents an abundance of choices—so many that it's tricky to see which is correct. Have you been mulling a big decision related to love or career? You may have to make a call soon and it won't be simple. Perhaps you have more than one job offer or love interest to choose from. It's possible you are being pulled along in a flight of fancy. Try to be objective and consider what the best decision might be for both the short and long term. What is your intuition telling you? Check in with your higher self before choosing the option that feels right. Ensure that you are doing everything you can to make the most informed decision.

Eight of Cups

KEYWORDS: Abandonment, withdrawal, escape

MEANING: Letting go There are times in our lives when walking away is the best option—the Eight of Cups is a reminder of this. Sometimes it is necessary to abandon a situation, person, or job. This can feel disappointing; you may question your strength and backbone. But it takes courage to recognize the right time to let go. You may feel weary now. It's time to explore what will bring you true happiness. While this card appears to indicate some soul-searching and a feeling of being cut adrift, take heart—know you have tried your best and there are times when you have to cut your losses.

Nine of Cups

KEYWORDS: Abundance, appreciation, wishes coming true

MEANING: Contentment The Nine of Cups is pure joy—happiness and wish-fulfillment encapsulated. When you're happy and you know it, clap your hands! Relationships, work, lifestyle, and wellbeing are blessed. If you are waiting for a wish to be granted, you should be beaming with satisfaction soon. Remember gratitude and to count your blessings. Do this and even more wishes will be granted soon. Dream jobs, the right romantic partner, the home you have always yearned for: all can be yours. Make sure you appreciate wonderful moments with friends and the people you care about. Revel in it and like will attract like. Let the good times roll!

Ten of Cups

KEYWORDS: Concord, blissful relationships, harmony

MEANING: Union The Ten of Cups can bring us the fairytale ending we crave. It represents an abundance of love and happiness, especially when it comes to happy families. Connecting and bonding are emphasized, as is appreciation of the love in your life. Romance, engagement, marriage, and starting a family are strongly highlighted by this card. It signifies meeting your soulmate and understanding how precious this is. It's time to follow your heart and ensure your life is being lived at its highest spiritual frequency, healing any hurt and replacing it with pure love.

Page of Cups

KEYWORDS: Joy, curiosity, possibility

MEANING: **Creativity** The Page of Cups is beckoning inspiration, brilliant ideas, fun, and creativity. Positive news is on the way. Keep an open mind—you never know what to expect with this card. It could also mean that someone will enter your life who will change the way you think—and lift your heart too. Remember that feeling when you were a kid and anything seemed possible? This is the energy that is being conjured up at the moment. Romance with someone young (or young at heart), thrilling gossip, new friendship, and positive outcomes for interviews and tests are all possibilities.

Knight of Cups

KEYWORDS: Romance, charm, imagination

MEANING: **Dreaming** The Knight of Cups is the romantic dreamer, the poet, the artist. You may have someone swooping into your life who fits this description. In terms of energy, you are being drawn to the beauty of life, idealism, harmony, and your best possible self and future. The question is, how can you make this a reality? It could be that you are called on to make a decision based on emotions rather than hard logic. Out-of-this-world romances may pop up in your life; there certainly is the feeling of being swept off one's feet. Career and money opportunities will be particularly enticing now, but make sure there is solid reality behind honeyed promises.

The Suit of Cups WATER

Queen of Cups

KEYWORDS: Compassion, intuition, serenity

MEANING: Sensitivity The Queen of Cups brings a lovely nurturing, maternal vibe. This may represent a person in your life, or about to enter it, who will be full of compassion and care for you—perhaps a relative, older friend, or colleague who will look after you and serve your best interests. Or perhaps you are harnessing these energies for others. This is a time to tap into your intuition; what will bring you contentment now is feelings and emotions, not cold logic. Even if others need your support, don't forget to replenish yourself spiritually so you don't feel drained. This card may be informing you of a pregnancy or a nurturing relationship. In career, it is guiding you into caring and healing—think counseling or nursing.

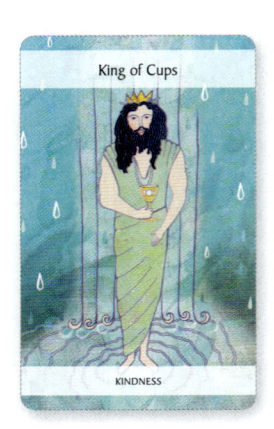

King of Cups

KEYWORDS: Emotion, sagacity, excitement

MEANING: Kindness The King of Cups is the figure who understands where the heart and the head meet. He can offer caring wisdom that understands your emotional needs as well as your practical concerns. A person like this, who is a good listener and mentor, may be entering your life as a teacher or spiritual advisor. Alternatively, this can indicate that you are discovering a balance between your head and your heart. This card represents the need for emotional maturity and healthy boundaries. You need to channel your energies to stay calm and firm, but also remain compassionate when others are getting hot under the collar. The King of Cups is reminding you that all will be well.